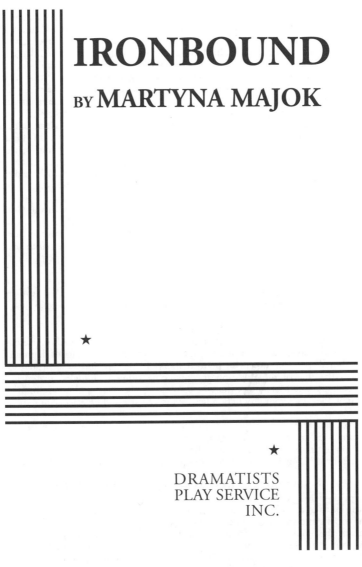

IRONBOUND

BY MARTYNA MAJOK

DRAMATISTS
PLAY SERVICE
INC.

IRONBOUND was originally produced at Round House Theatre Company (Ryan Rilette, Producing Artistic Director) in Bethesda, Maryland, as part of the Women's Voices Theater Festival, on September 9, 2015. It was directed by Daniella Topol, the scenic designer was James Kronzer, the costume designer was Kathleen C. Geldard, the lighting designers were Brian MacDevitt and Andrew R. Cissna, the sound designer was Eric Shimelonis, and the dramaturg was Jessica Pearson. The cast was as follows:

DARJA .... Alexandra Henrikson
TOMMY .... Jefferson A. Russell
MAKS .... Josiah Bania
VIC .... William Vaughan

The New York premiere of IRONBOUND was produced in March 2016 by Rattlestick Playwrights Theater (David Van Asselt, Artistic Director) and Women's Project Theater (Lisa McNulty, Producing Artistic Director; Maureen Moynihan, Managing Director). It was directed by Daniella Topol, the scenic and lighting designs were by Justin Townsend, the costume designer was Kaye Voyce, and the sound designer was Jane Shaw. The cast was as follows:

DARJA .... Marin Ireland
TOMMY .... Morgan Spector
MAKS .... Josiah Bania
VIC .... Shiloh Fernandez

IRONBOUND was developed by Steppenwolf Theatre Company (Martha Lavey, Artistic Director, David Hawkanson, Executive Director), through its New Play Initiative and was presented as part of its First Look Repertory of New Work at Steppenwolf Theatre Company, Chicago, IL. The play was the winner of the 2014 David Calicchio Emerging American Playwright Prize at Marin Theatre Company (Jasson Minadakis, Artistic Director; Michael Barker, Managing Director), Mill Valley, CA.

IRONBOUND was commissioned by a grant from the National New Play Network, with funding from the Smith Prize for New Plays.

PEOPLE

Darja.

[DAR-ya]

Tommy.

Maks.

Vic.

Darja and Tommy can be late 30s/early 40s.
Maks can be 30s.
Vic should appear teenage/early 20s.
The play spans 22 years. In 2006, Darja is 34.

PLACE

A bus stop at night, a quarter-mile from a factory in Elizabeth, NJ.
Or where there used to be a factory, depending on the year.

DIALOGISTICS

Slashes (//) indicate overlap.
Ellipses (…) are active silences.
Polish language is italicized. [Phonetics and translations can be found at the back of the book.]

A note on staging.
The play should be performed without an intermission.
Darja does not leave the stage until the very end of the play.

A note on performance.
It can be tempting to play the circumstances of these characters' lives and end up missing the comedy. It is my hope for an audience to laugh and understand.

A note on New Jersey:
The Jersey I know is gravel and cattails. Empty quarter drinks and Buds litter parking lots. A marsh, a highway, bridges. Almost everyone is from somewhere else. And, yes, there's a reason they're not living in New York.

There is an old story about a worker suspected of stealing:
every evening, as he leaves the factory,
the wheelbarrow he rolls in front of him is carefully inspected.
The guards can find nothing. It is always empty.
Finally, the penny drops:
what the worker is stealing are the wheelbarrows themselves.

—Slavoj Žižek, *Violence*

Now near the end of the middle stretch of road
What have I learned? Some earthly wiles. An art.
That often I cannot tell good fortune from bad,
That once had seemed so easy to tell apart.

—Robert Pinsky, "Jersey Rain"

IRONBOUND

Scene 1
2014. Winter.

A streetlight zaps on.

Night. An environment of black.
Stars exist beyond smog; we don't see them.
A bus stop. Perhaps a faded sign. But probably not.
This world is one of constant less.

The chill of winter is just starting to set in.

Two people fight. Darja in sweats, a scarf, and a hoodie—the clothes of a cleaning lady. She carries a large tote bag with her. Slavic accent. Tommy wears a Jersey Devils jacket over his postal worker's uniform. Shorts. A tribal calf tat.

DARJA. What you don't understand is how so much you // hurt me.
TOMMY. I'm sorry!
DARJA. And I suppose to do with this what? What I suppose to do with this?
TOMMY. What you need to realize is it was from a different time. A Different Time.
DARJA. It was four month ago.
TOMMY. And I'm different now. Get in the car.
DARJA. Four month you keep from me and how many times we, since you, how many?
TOMMY. Can you please fuckin please get in the fuckin car please?
DARJA. This was not the week. This was not good week to do this.
TOMMY. I didn't do it this week. This week's the week you chose to find out about it.
Just get in the car. Yer not ridin that bus.

DARJA. I rode the other bus here.

TOMMY. And I tailed you in my—and that bus was not *this* bus, was not *this* neighborhood, waitin in *this*.

DARJA. I was riding that bus whole the time. Since that factory open, I ride.

TOMMY. O wow *that's* the factory you used to work at—?

DARJA. We are not having nice conversation now. The past. Memories. No.

TOMMY. *(Trying.)* What happened to it // again?

DARJA. No.

…

TOMMY. Okay. Y'know what, Darja? What you gotta understand, man, is that people fuck up. It's planned that way. Yer Catholic. You know. It's planned this way for people to fuck up cuz if we were all perfect, fuck, who'd need to be Catholic. It's a cycle a system listen: We're not in control of these things, okay? Okay? We are Outta Control. And if you wanna crossify me for one little, man, after *everything* we've, everything *I've* done, for you, how many years?, if you wanna do that, Darja, then… I don't know, man. I just don't think you should do that, Darja.

> *(Longer than it should take:)*

I'm sorry.

DARJA. Me too.

Also you have no idea what you talking about, also.

TOMMY. The bus won't come. It's too late.

DARJA. And with rich lady, hey. Congratulation to you.

TOMMY. Did you hear me?

DARJA. It will come.

TOMMY. Fine, it comes, then what? You get off at Market and, what, walk? Yer gonna walk through Newark now? A woman like you?

DARJA. I do this many year before you, Tommy. A woman like what.

TOMMY. Get in the car.

DARJA. No.

TOMMY. DARJA GET IN THE FUCKIN CAR.

…

DARJA. You are not the one what gets to curse.

TOMMY. We're goin to the same place.

DARJA. And I pack when I get there.

TOMMY. Yer not gonna—

DARJA. No. You pack.

TOMMY. I'm not goin—
DARJA. No. Me. I am going.
TOMMY. Yeah? With what car?
DARJA. HEY! I had car.
TOMMY. Well you don't now, do you.
...
DARJA. I will find someone. I will find someone else.
TOMMY. Where?
DARJA. I found *you*. I was not blind person. I was not stupid. I know exactly what was I doing so I was not stupid. I weighed you on scale and I say mm Okay.
TOMMY. "Okay"?
DARJA. I am forty-two years old, married-twice-already woman: I have no time for stupid. So I weigh you on scale. Okay? So tell me, Tommy. How many times you—
TOMMY. What good's that kinda information?
DARJA. How many?
TOMMY. Why?
DARJA. Five? Four? One time every month?
TOMMY. Why do you need to know?
DARJA. Is some numbers I can handle. And some I probably cannot.
...
TOMMY. If you leave, I don't know what's gonna happen to me.
DARJA. Five?
TOMMY. I'm not good alone, you know that.
DARJA. Five?
...
TOMMY. Five.
DARJA. Not nine?
...
TOMMY. Nine.
DARJA. Not twelve?
TOMMY. No.
DARJA. Not twelve?
TOMMY. No.
DARJA. Not fourteen?
...
TOMMY. No.
DARJA. You look in my face and you lie. Why you lie my face when I find out things so good?

9

TOMMY. You never made a mistake?

DARJA. Fourteen times it's not // mistake—

TOMMY. —A very // big mistake—

DARJA. —Fourteen times it's career.

Just answer me one thing. You want me I stay?

TOMMY. Yes. Yes, of course I, yes.

DARJA. Why.

TOMMY. I love you.

DARJA. NO. WE ARE NOT HAVING NICE CONVERSATION.

TOMMY. Well, you wanna know why, that's why.

DARJA. You love me, okay, but you consider leaving. You, so obvious, you consider this—

TOMMY. I didn't *plan* // like— Things Happen.

DARJA. I TALK NOW.

Must be something what scares you more than leaving and so you stay. People imagine things. Things what can happen them, alone. In nights, they make pictures this thing in their heads. What you imagine? For me, is when I am cleaning her house and—

TOMMY. Does she know you know? About—that you know?

DARJA. What good would be if she know? I need job. And she have—*you* know—very dirty house.

No. She don't know.

You have broke me to one hundred pieces.

TOMMY. I'm sorry. How much you want me to apologize? I apologized. So much. It's in the past.

DARJA. What you imagine?

…

TOMMY. It's the nights. At the apartment. When yer workin late and no one's home. Yer always workin. And late.

There's no sound.

And thoughts come.

I'm not good alone. You know that.

DARJA. And what happens if you can't fill apartment with someone?

TOMMY. I could find someone. But it's not about findin *some*one.

DARJA. Yes this is.

TOMMY. No. No, it's not. It's about *you* not leavin.

DARJA. Where? Where you would find someone? In *post office*? Go to someone's house? Slip to them *letter*? Slide in their mail slot your letter? "Meet me tonight."

TOMMY. I never slipped her a letter.

DARJA. Did I say you did?

TOMMY. That's not even my route. Montclair. Not my postal route.

...

If you think about it... I'm the best you ever had.

...

DARJA. This stupid bus. I am walking.

TOMMY. I'll just tail you, you start walkin. HEY!—

(She has set out. He grabs her arm, stops her.)

Don't be fuckin crazy.

Okay?

Get in the car.

DARJA. Or you will just hold me like this until what?

(A moment.
He lets go.
A breath.)

What if I did to you what you did to me? What if?

TOMMY. I'd stay with you. And forgive you. And love you so very very much.

DARJA. You would stay with me, yes sure. Yes sure, because I make easy your life. For you, I cook, I clean, I lay there for you. I make sounds. Easy life. And you can whatever you want because I will lay there. Of course you would stay with me.

TOMMY. That's what you think?

DARJA. I weigh you on scale.

TOMMY. Well that's not what I think.

And, actually, you lay there very loudly.

Yer welcome.

DARJA. No, you are welcome.

Everything can change. You come home one day and maybe it's no one there.

Everything it's already changed.

So what you will give me now?

TOMMY. What?

DARJA. What you will *give* me. For me to stay. Because you love me. So very very much.

You think you can whatever you want with whoever you want for one night. One hour. Ten minutes (I know you). But everyone goes their homes after.

TOMMY. What is this "everyone" shit? It was One Person.

11

DARJA. And I know she have her home, her kid, her husband—rich husband—to go after. But you? What you have?

(Tommy inhales to reply.
No response.)

Okay. So what you will give?

…

TOMMY. I could… try to be more understanding—

DARJA. No. These it's fake ideas. Concrete, I need. Concrete. I need How Much You Will Give.

TOMMY. How much what?

DARJA. I need figures. Numbers. Money.
You are not my great love, okay? You are not my great love for talking to me fake ideas.

TOMMY. Yer mine. Yer my great—

DARJA. We are not having nice conversation! I can't trust "understanding." I can't trust "try." I can trust three thousand dollars in my hands.

TOMMY. Three thousand?!?

DARJA. Dollars. In my bank. It's number I can trust.

TOMMY. Three thousand?

DARJA. At least.

…

TOMMY. So I give you three grand and you do what with it?

DARJA. Pay bills.

TOMMY. Not a car? Not buy a car?

DARJA. Maybe. Maybe I buy car.

TOMMY. You have no idea where he is.

…

DARJA. Does not matter what I buy.

TOMMY. It does if yer gonna take my money and run.

DARJA. You have three thousand dollars?

TOMMY. That's not the point.

DARJA. I think point is if you want me I stay or no. You have no kids, no house, one credit card. Car payments and rent you have.

TOMMY. The *majority* of rent.

DARJA. That it's all you have. I buy, I make, all your food. Laundry. Birth control! Birth control it's costing! How nice this is, only worry for yourself, no kids, just pay // for yourself—

TOMMY. Aleks is twenty-five years—

DARJA. Two! Two! Aleks is twenty-two! It's two twos, how hard this is?

12

TOMMY. Twenty-anything, in my mind, makes you a grown-ass man. If he wants to go, he's gonna go. And he's gone.

DARJA. He it's not okay to go! You have three thousand dollars. You have more than three thousand dollars. What is for you three thousand dollars? Nothing. Is nothing for you.

...

I will come back. Okay?

TOMMY. You have no idea where he is.

DARJA. That's why I need three thousand shit dollars! I need one thousand for car so I can go find him and two thousand maybe for whatever he needs.

TOMMY. Rehab?

DARJA. Whatever he needs.

TOMMY. I told you I'm not payin for some deadbeat's kid.

DARJA. No, you paying me. You paying me to make noise.

TOMMY. You know how much rehab costs? Cuz that's what that kid needs.

DARJA. I can find something for cheap. Listen, you have broke me to millions pieces. You take my last good years I have in my life—

TOMMY. You were thirty-five when we got together.

DARJA. And you know how shit were the first thirty-five. You don't wanna pay for my son, Tommy?, okay, it's fine. So just you pay for me and what money I make, I pay for my son. That's Fine. I say Fine to this before, I say Fine now. And right now I need car.

TOMMY. I'm not payin you to find him. So he can, fuckin, steal from me, trash our place. No, please, I'd love to see the cops again. Reconnect. I'd fuckin love it.

DARJA. For work, I need money for car.

TOMMY. No. If I give you money, I'd be payin you to stay. I mean I'd help *support* you. I'm not *payin* you like a, I'm not *payin* you. This would be me offerin you support. Cuz you know what, D? I respect you. You work hard. I respect you. It's not your fault where you were born. It's not your fault you were dealt a shit hand. All those Communists'n Nazis'n shit. But you came here. Home of the brave. Make a better—home of the brave! Even if you knew you'd be behind, you came. And that?: Respect. That, from me, gets you respect. So if you need money, I can give you money. I can help you out. Not much, not three thousand dollars. But you'd need to stay.

...

DARJA. How much?

TOMMY. See, this is terrible right here. This is a terrible thing to talk about.

DARJA. How much or I am moving tomorrow.

TOMMY. You always threaten to move.

DARJA. And you listen then.

TOMMY. You never do.

DARJA. This time it's different.

TOMMY. Fine. Okay, fine, but for one mistake? For one mistake you'd trash it all?

DARJA. I counted seventeen times in four months with her. One time in 2013. Three in 2012, but this was someone else. "Allison." And in 2011, this was also someone else. "Courtney." And this is only counting times I know you go to meet with them.

Your phone has tap.

Since I know something is going on, it's have tap.

I listen every Monday to what I collect. While I clean Linda's house.

…

TOMMY. I put a password on my phone.

DARJA. Your mother's birthday. Backwards. Her birthday backwards.

…

TOMMY. You can't tap a cell—

DARJA. There is app.

…

…

TOMMY. So you know… how much exactly?

DARJA. I start in 2010. I start collecting things I can hold in my hands then.

TOMMY. And you waited till now.

DARJA. I was tired of lying.

TOMMY. Why'd you wait till now?

DARJA. I am tired of you lying.

…

…

TOMMY. You were holdin on to it? To tellin me you knew? For, what, for a rainy fuckin day?

DARJA. You pay or no?

TOMMY. Aleks left. He—

DARJA. No, // this is not about—

TOMMY. —he's never left before. He'd fuck shit up. Plenty. Torment you. Me. But he never left. So you were waitin, huh?

Till, what, till you needed a trump? Till you really needed a fuckin bailout?

DARJA. This is just the situation.

TOMMY. He makes you cry.

DARJA. What?

TOMMY. Worse than I ever seen in a woman. Why you hold on to him, he makes you fuckin cry?

...

DARJA. Two thousand. Just for car.

TOMMY. I don't do that. I don't make you cry.

DARJA. Just one thousand even.

TOMMY. I don't steal your car and run off for, how many, three days?, without a call. So you gotta take two buses to work. In this fuckin—wasteland. I don't do that.

Shoulda tapped *his* phone, huh?

...

DARJA. Okay.

I leave you tomorrow.

TOMMY. Yeah? When the bus comes? Where's yer bus?

...

Huh, Darja? Where's yer bus?

...

DARJA. Just one thousand.

Tommy.

Seventeen times. In four months.

You owe me so much more than just one thousand.

TOMMY. I have pictures of you.

I have pictures of you doin things. To me. I have the video. Remember the video? I said I erased it. I have it.

I could show it to people.

You can start makin demands when you got a leg to stand on.

Get in the car.

DARJA. *("Nice try.")* No one here knows me.

Show them.

(A challenge.) No one in this country knows me.

...

Just—just one thousand?

Scene 2
1992. Summer.

The sound of cicadas.

Darja and Maks. They wear shirts with sleeves, rolled up. Uniforms. Tags. Sweat stains. A hot night. Maks is from the same country as Darja.

They count out their change. This is their game. Taking turns, they put forward one coin from their respective pockets. That's one coin per turn. Before them rests a small mass of coins.

Darja takes out a coin from her pocket, places it. Then Maks takes out a coin from his pocket, places it. And so the game goes. The winner gets a sexual favor tonight.

MAKS. Five.
DARJA. … Ten.
MAKS. Twenty.
DARJA. Fourteen-five!
MAKS. Mm. Forty.
DARJA. What?
MAKS. *Forty*-five.
DARJA. *("You jerk.")* Yes yes. Forty-five. Twenty, thirty, forty, yes okay.
MAKS. Fifty.
DARJA. Sixty.
MAKS. Eighty… five.
DARJA. One… ten.
MAKS. One… fifteen.
DARJA. Uh oh. Close.
…
One… twenty.

MAKS. One twenty… one.
…
DARJA. Twenty-six!
MAKS. *(Disbelief.) No, kurdy…*
DARJA. I win! One twenty-six!
MAKS. No no, bus is costing more in nights.
DARJA. No no, I win!
MAKS. Yes yes. You win.
DARJA. Pay up.
MAKS. Now, pay up?
DARJA. I don't see anyone.
MAKS. Really? Now? Here?
DARJA. Do you see anyone…

> *(He gets down on his knees. She's loving this.)*

MAKS. *Dobra, to dziś zrobię Ci coś //* co—
DARJA. You have to practice—
MAKS. So tonight I—

> *(He rides his hands up her thighs.)*

Roztopię Cię, kobieto—
DARJA. Practice—
MAKS. I don't know how to say in English—
DARJA. Say: Tonight you make me happy.
MAKS. Tonight—
DARJA. Because I win.
MAKS. Because you win, tonight I make you // happy.
DARJA. Tonight you make me happy.
MAKS. *(Fifth time this week.)* Again.
DARJA. *("Damn right.")* Again.
MAKS. *("Damn right indeed.")* Again.
DARJA. *(Pure joy.)* Again!
MAKS. You are too good this game.
DARJA. *You* are too good for me not to be this good this game.

> *(They kiss.*
> *A car passes by, honks at them, trying to be funny.*
> *They both flip it the bird, without taking their mouths off*
> *each other.)*

You think rich people have this games?
MAKS. They have other kinds games, rich people.

(They kiss. Just a little too long.)

DARJA. *Maksiu*, wait.

Tonight it's special night.

MAKS. *(Still holding her, kissing her neck.)* Yeeeeaaahh it is.

DARJA. No no… I mean *yes* but… I have something tonight to tell you.

Look in my bag.

MAKS. Right now?

DARJA. Right now.

MAKS. … Right now?

DARJA. Right now!

> *(He looks in her tote bag.*
> *Looks at her.*
> *Looks at bag.*
> *Looks at her.)*

MAKS. You buy this?

DARJA. You funny.

MAKS. You…

DARJA. … rent this. Just for tonight. For special night.

(Maks pulls out a delicate nightgown.)

MAKS. From who?

DARJA. From woman I work for.

MAKS. Woman you, the crazy? She it's one hundred years old woman, why you want this. And she it's crazy.

DARJA. She it's sick.

MAKS. She it's sick with crazy.

DARJA. She it's not wearing this. This it's from when she's just married, when she was nineteen years old. *I* am just married and I am *twenty* so really I am late to have something like this. I find in some box with tape on whole this thing. These people always are throwing beautiful things. She can't to throw this beautiful thing. Look at this.

(He feels the nightgown. Flower petals.)

Is just for tonight. She will never know.

MAKS. What if she does?

DARJA. … She it's crazy.

Is just for this night.

MAKS. *She* it's crazy?

DARJA. You talking so much. You will not be talking so much tonight.

(*She models it against herself.*)

Maksiu.

MAKS. Bring this back.

DARJA. Why?

MAKS. I want you wear something what's for you.

DARJA. And this it's not for me?

MAKS. It's, no, this it's not for you, you stole this.

DARJA. So, okay, I give this back. After tonight.

MAKS. *No, Darju, ty nie rozumiesz—*

DARJA. English.

MAKS. (*Dismissal.*) Ah.

DARJA. You will never go no place you don't speak English.

MAKS. Yeah? I speak English whole time am here. Since I come here, I speak English. You know who else speaks English? Whole rest this country. Is nothing special you speak English this country. You don't *take* things like some bullshit person. Bring this back.

...

I buy for you one.

One day.

(*They stand in silence.*
Then he takes out liquor. Swigs.)

You want?

DARJA. No.

MAKS. Now you mad?

DARJA. I just don't want drink.

MAKS. Why?

DARJA. I just don't.

MAKS. You steal but you don't drink. What sense is this.

DARJA. Why that is not for me?

MAKS. You did not buy it.

DARJA. What if she give to me this?

MAKS. She did not give to you that.

DARJA. She throw this away, same thing like if she give me. I am wearing her clothes sometimes. When I push her in wheelchair, I wear her hats so if she turn around her head, I can fast take this off. When I shop for her food, I wear her scarf. When I take her bills to post office. Sometimes I even walk in Central Park—just for like,

19

little bit—in her dress. Beautiful dress. Blue. I take this off before I go inside and clean her furnitures. But people on the street... in life... they for some reason they always know who am I. I wear her clothes but.
Maks.
Why you think we look poor?
MAKS. Because we don't look rich.
You wait. You have one day rich husband.
DARJA. You are divorcing me?
MAKS. You are not funny.
DARJA. Yes I am.

> *(He takes out a cigarette, lights.)*

MAKS. Want?
DARJA. No.
MAKS. No?
DARJA. No.
MAKS. No?
DARJA. No.
...
MAKS. No?
DARJA. No!
MAKS. Who are you?
DARJA. Is too hot.
MAKS. To smoke is?
DARJA. Too hot to smoke, yes.
MAKS. You okay maybe?
DARJA. I am fine thank you very much and yourself?
MAKS. *("Suit yourself.")* Okay.

> *(He smokes.*
> *They stare out, waiting for the bus.)*

Late, yes?
DARJA. *(Terrified; taken aback.)* What?
...
MAKS. The bus.
Late.
Yes?
...
DARJA. Yes.
Late.

The bus.

    (Maks smokes.)

I love this smell.
MAKS. You can have one.
DARJA. No. I can't.
MAKS. Why you can't?
DARJA. No.
…
MAKS. This waiting is bullshit. I want car.
DARJA. Yes.
MAKS. One day.
DARJA. I want house.
MAKS. Maybe.
DARJA. You don't want house?
MAKS. I want to know we can go any place we want.
DARJA. *(Not smiling.)* Chicago?
MAKS. *(Smiling.)* Chicago!
DARJA. Please don't do it.

    (Too late. Maks has taken out his harmonica.
    He plays.
    He sings the chorus of "Czerwony Jak Cegła" by Dżem—a
    Polish blues song.)

    (He's damn good. He shines.)

    (Darja, however, is having none of it.
    This feels like the 500th time he is doing this.)

MAKS. *(Singing.)*
    Czerwony jak cegła—
DARJA. *(This always happens.)* Okay.
MAKS. *(Singing.)*
    —rozgrzany jak piec,
    Muszę mieć, // muszę ją mieć—
DARJA. Yeah okay.
MAKS.
    Czerwony jak cegła,
    rozgrzany jak piec,
    Fuck this bus,
    Oh yeeeeaaaaahhhh, fuck this bus.

    (He plays, takes her, gets her to dance. She enjoys it in spite of

herself. He finds his way into her hair, her neck. Turns into a
close, slow dance. He sings or hums the song slower, into her.
It's wonderful.
Then she slips out of the dance.)

DARJA. Yes, very nice. You sing very nice. Not like most nice in whole the world but nice.

MAKS. Me and Clinton, we will play together one day.

DARJA. Amazing: The Wall falls down; American dream falls in. Everyone thinks they can be star now. Amazing.

MAKS. It's only American, dreams?

DARJA. Blues it's American.

MAKS. Okay and but this song they write in Poland so.

DARJA. No one understands you.

MAKS. They will understand. It's blues. It's Chicago.

DARJA. There it's black people there play blues, Chicago.

MAKS. See?, so I can be like, New Thing.
Sing.

DARJA. I am not singer.

MAKS. No, you are not singer but you can sing. All people can sing. You can't sing means you are died.

DARJA. I work in factory. That it's what I do. And I clean old woman.

MAKS. And steal her clothes. You can't tell me you don't want more.

DARJA. I do. Yes, Maks. I do, very much, want more.

MAKS. Okay so this is why we go Chicago. I can spend whole my life in this place lifting, pushing. But one song? Good song? And you know all good music it's come from poor people.

DARJA. And if this don't work?

MAKS. What?

DARJA. Your one song?
Good song?

(This is the first time she's voiced this.)

MAKS. It just will.

DARJA. And what we will do now?

MAKS. Why it's all this questions?

DARJA. I just think we should think.

MAKS. Think what.

DARJA. Think if maybe… think what if maybe… in case…

MAKS. What.

DARJA. We need more money.

MAKS. Because you want, what, things like this? *(Re: nightgown.)*
DARJA. We can't live always like how we live now. We need money.
Now.
MAKS. Okay but what more I can do? I speak English. I have job
and I work this all the time.
And I am beautiful.
DARJA. What this means, you—
MAKS. So in America, if you beautiful, they give to you jobs. Take
two people, put them next each other, both speak English, and,
see?, our boss he take the beautiful. You can never be ugly or we will
starve. Or fat. Never also be fat.
DARJA. Ania it's not beautiful—not anymore— and she have job.
Ania lose her arm and she have job. Is *because* she have job that she
lose her arm. And *because* she lose her arm, she keep job. Funny
mathematics.
MAKS. *("Stop talking, maybe that's enough for now.")* Okay—
DARJA. You see her? They take skin from her here *(Re: stomach.)*
this skin they take to make the arm again. I see her... how she say
this... button. I see her button on her new arm when she shake
hands.
MAKS. But she get money. They take care of this.
DARJA. She get money but not so much money. Not like, what
this costs to have arm. And she get to keep her job in factory.
With us. Hoorah.
MAKS. *(Looking around.)* Okay, *może teraz nie jest // najlepszy czas—*
DARJA. Anyone here it's Polish so who you think you keeping
secrets from speaking Polish?
MAKS. Okay. You know what? Maybe you forget how should you
act with me.
DARJA. Maybe you too you forget. You want to be big man? Have
me act to you like you big man? Okay. So I want more, Maks. I need
insurance. Apartment. *Out* of basement apartment. Car. I want car.
MAKS. Okay.
One day.
DARJA. I want more than anything car.
MAKS. Then this is sad life.
DARJA. There will one day be when you have to put away this songs.

> *(Maks lights another cigarette.)*

Don't smoke this by me.
MAKS. You said you "love."

DARJA. I don't want smoke by me.
MAKS. So don't make me mad, I don't smoke.
This it's what you have tonight to tell me? How much I don't give you? Thank you.
Thank you so very much.

(*They stand silent.*)

Is music in my head right now. You should know this. And this it's what I do when bus it's late or when someone skin it's rip from bones. Or my wife she say to me am nothing.
Don't try to take this from me.

(*They stand apart a little while longer. Facing forward.*
Then she moves to him. Rests against him, holds his hand,
wraps it around her waist.
But something doesn't quite fit.
They stare forward.)

Is good to have thing like this. For some reason you think is bad but is good. I watch people. Singers. Not here because we don't go places but... home. I watch faces them when they sing. They look... pain sometimes. Eyes closed. Mouth big, red. And maybe you don't see this but what I see it's... it's something in them... when they sing... it's like escaping them. Something leaves their mouth what makes inside them red, what burns. Is something hot, something loud, something maybe bad.
Think what things he maybe do if he could not get this out.
Something maybe bad.
I come from shit, okay?, and I—
DARJA. And me?
MAKS. And we come *to* shit. But we have something. We are not just body. Lift. Pull. Push. We are more than this.
DARJA. Well no one pays us for this "more."
MAKS. You can burn money. Gone, two seconds. Money it's nothing. Is important. But is nothing. What's most important in this life it's this thing you have what no one can take from you.
DARJA. I can't think what's something can't someone take.
MAKS. Then you make one. One thing what's yours in whole this world. People try to take, you fight.
DARJA. I am fighting.
MAKS. Cars break.
...

I have music. People need to know this.

DARJA. *I* know this.

MAKS. People in this country need to know this so I don't fall from this world like nothing ever happen.

DARJA. I know this. And I know you. I know only you here. In whole country. In whole country, really, I have only you.

MAKS. And is many things can happen to me.

...

Don't try to take this from me.

(He smokes. She watches him.)

...

DARJA. We need money this week. Little extra.

MAKS. Because see?, again money. Whole this time we talk, it's money.

DARJA. This week, we need.

And maybe for few months.

MAKS. Why.

DARJA. To go to doctor.

...

MAKS. You feel sick?

DARJA. No.

...

...

...

> *(Maks knows.*
> *He looks at her.*
> *Looks forward.*
> *A worried face.*
> *They look forward.)*

...

There is the bus.

Scene 3
2014. Winter.

Headlights.

A car horn blares from a distance. Closer. Closer. A car skids. Stops.

Car door opens, slams shut.

Tommy enters in his postal uniform, frazzled.

TOMMY. The fuck's the matter with you!?!
DARJA. You were not stopping.
TOMMY. What if I didn't see you? It's fuckin dark out!
DARJA. You have your lights.
TOMMY. The fuck is your problem?
DARJA. You are happy you did not hit me?

    (Tommy catches his breath.)

TOMMY. I coulda // fuckin—
DARJA. I know what you could. Calm down. Everything it's okay. How are you?
TOMMY. Are you fuckin kidding?
DARJA. Calm down.
TOMMY. Why were you standin in the middle of the road?!
DARJA. I know which way you come home.
TOMMY. And you couldn't just see me at home?
DARJA. You pass me in your car, standing this bus stop, two nights, and you never stop to give me ride.
TOMMY. You said you didn't want one, made that pretty clear.
DARJA. AND SO WHAT THE FUCK IS WRONG WITH YOU FOR LISTENING.
…
How… how damnit are you, is why I stop you, how are you. Two days already we don't talk, no hello when I come home, nothing. So. How are you.
TOMMY. This how you apologize?

26

DARJA. Who apologize?, *me?*
TOMMY. *(Moving to exit back to car.)* Right.
DARJA. TOMMY HOW ARE YOU.
TOMMY. *(Turning back.)* I'M HUNGRY. I JUST FINISHED WORK.
DARJA. WHAT YOU WOULD LIKE FOR DINNER.
TOMMY. Are we playin now?
...
I got plans for dinner. I was goin home to change.
DARJA. Where you going?
TOMMY. Some Italian place.
DARJA. Which one?
TOMMY. No.
DARJA. With "Linda"?
TOMMY. My new password's good, right?
Yes. With Linda.
DARJA. Mm. Linda. It's fancy?
TOMMY. You jumped in fronta my car for a restaurant recommendation?
DARJA. Sure why not?, since you expert.
TOMMY. Look if you got a problem with what I'm doin, you can leave. You can pack and leave like you keep threatenin to—
DARJA. I don't want to leave.
TOMMY. You want *me* to leave then?
DARJA. No.
TOMMY. You know what I'm doin, you don't want me to leave?
DARJA. No.
TOMMY. You gonna ask me questions, where I'm goin, what Italian place?
DARJA. No. ... Am just—
TOMMY. What? You gonna come there and, fuckin, mace her, what?
DARJA. No.
TOMMY. Assault her?, I know you.
DARJA. No. Am just...
curious.
I like to
imagine. Just curious.
What you will eat?
TOMMY. I don't know yet. *(Really thinks about this a second.)* Pasta.
DARJA. Why you ask I would do this? Why you think I could be

27

like this? Mean like this? I am not like this. Violence. I don't "mace" people.

TOMMY. Fine. Yer right.

DARJA. I find other things to do to people.

…

TOMMY. What did you do?

DARJA. Did you know I lose all of them?

TOMMY. Wait, what did you do?

DARJA. All my houses, I lose. All my jobs. She call to every woman I work for. Every one. She tell to them I "damage." I "damage" things. Yeah okay but what she did not to tell them is why, why I "damage" things.

TOMMY. Did you do something to Linda?

DARJA. Not to her, to stupid her. Her things. Her clothes. The bras, the underwears. Dresses. // Few dresses.

TOMMY. Darja.

DARJA. And I drink her wine. The most dusty one.

TOMMY. What did you do to her things?

DARJA. What you think, I burn them.

TOMMY. Like, up? You burned them up?

DARJA. Yes, up. Away. No more.

TOMMY. The woman's a damn millionaire // and you just burned her shit up?

DARJA. Her *husband* it's millionaire and // she it's sick nasty inside his house—

TOMMY. Jesus fuckin— Is it still burning?

DARJA. Was beautiful. And so was her clothes. You know I think first maybe I keep all this things but then I think No. I don't know what she does in this things. Dirty dirty nasty sick.

She want I clean her house?

I clean the bitch's house.

(Darja finds this hilarious. Until she doesn't.
Tommy watches a woman laugh about arson.)

TOMMY. This is hilarious to you?

DARJA. Tommy, I have no job!

TOMMY. Did you think you would?

DARJA. I have NO job!

TOMMY. Welcome to America. Get another one.

(At some point, Tommy takes out his phone to make a call.)

DARJA. How? Please tell to me how. You see peoples here they go to school years, *years* they go, and they don't have nothing now. What I can do? Even the ugly jobs they don't have no more. Look there. Look the factory there. Just empty and glass. No factories here, nothing. No car. What I can do?

TOMMY. Maybe you shoulda sold her fuckin shit instead of burnin it.

...

DARJA. You know what?

Yes.

Yes, fuck. Yes, I should.

TOMMY. Prob'ly insured.

DARJA. Damnit fuck.

(Darja, a little lost in the sobering reality of it all, looks at the rubble of the factory but speaks to Tommy, who is dealing with his phone.)

These people, if they could, they would send they houses to China to be cleaned. But we work till day our body breaks. Till place close or I close, I work and I barely—

TOMMY. *(On the phone, leaving a sexy message.)* Hey yeah it's the uh, The Pool Guy. Callin about yer uh, pool. Just callin to check in uh *confirm* that I'm still doin yer pool. Tonight. *(Extra sexy.)* Call me back.

(He hangs up. Darja looks at him.)

DARJA. Tommy—

TOMMY. Listen, I don't exactly owe you anything. Except rent. I owe you half the rent while we're still livin together and I left it on the table this morning—

(She kisses him abruptly.
He doesn't move away.
But he doesn't respond much either.)

DARJA. What time you are meeting her?

TOMMY. I got time. A little time.

DARJA. You could drive any other different way back home. But you drive here. By my bus.

Where I stand.

TOMMY. This is just the way home.

29

DARJA. You came out the car.
You try to make me jealous? Hm, Pool Guy?
TOMMY. Why, *are* you jealous? Firestarter?
…

…
DARJA. So how you are doing?
TOMMY. Good. Considering. Good.
…
… And yourself?
DARJA. Good.
Considering.
…
And work?
TOMMY. Oh work is—you know.
DARJA. They are, maybe they are, hiring? At… at post—?
TOMMY. No. I don't think so, no. Budget Cuts. Budget cuts all
over the place. People don't mail.
I'm lucky to still, y'know. Fuckin Internet.
DARJA. Yes.
TOMMY. Fuckin email.
DARJA. Yes.

> *(She kisses him again. Maybe it's more of a mutual one this time.)*

I can make pasta.
Let's go home.

> *(Tommy considers. He sees what she's doing. And is conflicted.
> He softly extricates himself from her embrace. It's not easy for
> him to ask her this.)*

TOMMY. You think yer gonna stay at the apartment?
DARJA. I—what?
I, yes, I think I should have enough. Maybe. For next month.
But maybe you can just—
TOMMY. I mean, after. Like will you be there after next month.
After the lease's up.
DARJA. I have to.
TOMMY. You have to?
DARJA. Yes, I have to.
TOMMY. "In case he comes back"?
DARJA. He it's not picking up my calls.
If Aleks comes back, I should be there.

TOMMY. You go to the police?

DARJA. Yes.

TOMMY. Missing kid or stolen car?

DARJA. Missing kid.

TOMMY. Shoulda told 'em stolen car.

DARJA. I miss // him—

TOMMY. The *car's* never fucked you over.

...

DARJA. I miss him very much.

...

TOMMY. Listen I'm sorry for what I'm about to but, I kinda, gotta since it's just a few, weeks really till we gotta decide about the, listen. Can you afford the rent?

DARJA. I said I think I—

TOMMY. On yer own?

DARJA. Why.

TOMMY. Cuz look I'm not gonna throw you out—

DARJA. Why you would throw me out.

TOMMY. I said I wouldn't, I would Not Throw You Out. But—

DARJA. What.

TOMMY. Just. Can you afford rent?

DARJA. ... Yes. Somehow. Maybe. Tommy, I don't have car so where I can go anyway, how I can move.

TOMMY. There's vans. Trucks.

DARJA. Yeah okay, what money I have for, and I have things, big things what are mine in the apartment.

TOMMY. Not that many. The furniture's mine.

DARJA. What you try to do?

TOMMY. I need to know whether to start lookin for a place or—

DARJA. Why you look for place?

TOMMY. Y'know what, I'll just start lookin for a place. I don't need that extra room. Save a few that way. I'll just look and you can tell me what you wanna do. Or tell Jim. You can talk to Jim about the lease.

DARJA. Why it's lease? Why money? Furniture, numbers. Why these things, all these *things*?

TOMMY. As opposed to what?

31

DARJA. To… more.

TOMMY. More what?

DARJA. Okay. Okay. You are playing now.

TOMMY. I don't know what yer talkin about, "more." You tap my phone. You destroy my girlfriend's shit—

DARJA. Girlfriend?

TOMMY. And you freeload.

So more what. What more is it you want?

DARJA. I don't know.

TOMMY. Well. If you don't know, I don't know.

DARJA. My second husband would say this.

TOMMY. He talked? I thought he'd just beat the shit out of you.

…

I'm sorry. I'm sorry I'm bein a fuckin jerk. I just, I can't have you fuckin shit up for me.

DARJA. Like what?

TOMMY. If what we had was different, you and me—

DARJA. We're together six almost seven years.

TOMMY. *Livin* together, we been, for six almost seven years.

DARJA. And so that's just nothing?

TOMMY. I dunno. You tell me. Was that a real kiss?

Was that you kissin me fer real there or puttin in an application fer the post office?

DARJA. For real, Tommy.

TOMMY. Yeah well I dunno. There's just some shit now, with us, that I don't know.

DARJA. And so what it's this with "Linda" now you have? This is real?

TOMMY. I don't know exactly.

Yet.

But I'd like to find out. She's not happy in her marriage and we // been—

DARJA. *("That's enough.")* Okay.

("You fucking idiot.") Okay.

…

(Sees he's serious.) Okay.

TOMMY. You don't hafta tell me now but, just lemme know what you wanna do. About the apartment.

Okay?

Sorry.

(He looks at her.
She's looking away. At the factory.)

DARJA. There was once woman at that factory—
TOMMY. Darja.
DARJA. They close this factory. First people they go or they let go and now they just, everything from China so—
TOMMY. Yeah that happens. Listen, I gotta // get goin—
DARJA. I can be fast. Six, almost seven years... And then you... and then you can...

There was woman. My friend. She was my friend. She, one day, she gets her sleeve catch in machine. It's paper factory and she work on one machine we use to cut papers. And this machine it slice her arm like paper. Layers. Like paper. The bone is left.

They tell to us, first day, they say we be careful this machine. They tell to us we be *so* careful, we must be scared this machine. It can do many things to us. We must be scared always so we do not sleep and nothing happens us.

It was so loud in this place, we wear plugs our ears. So when she was screaming...

We do not hear her.

No one hears.

I ask her how she could let this to happen to her. How she can forget to be scared.

She say me she could not remember what she was thinking... but she remembers for one moment she was thinking *something*.

She don't tell to me what this was. But I know.

She was thinking being not here.

She was thinking some place, something, what was not for her. Or she would see when her sleeve it's catching and her arm it's taking. Because that's where she is, she is here. Like me.

I am not good person. I am not good person also. I don't know who I think I am to say to you things. I don't know why I judge you. And you help me before. You help me before in bad times. After my second husband. After he...

I don't know how I will make it next month. How I will... And if I have to move... I... I don't know what to do. Truly. I... I don't know.

I am sorry. I am sorry for that I do bad things to you.

(Longer than it should take.)

I love you very much.

…

TOMMY. I gotta go.
DARJA. Can we go to dinner?
TOMMY. I'm already goin to dinner.
DARJA. Tomorrow?
TOMMY. I'm gonna keep seein this woman.
DARJA. …
TOMMY. I'm not gonna stop.
DARJA. …
TOMMY. I like her.

…

That doesn't bother you?

…

…

DARJA. No.
Just maybe sometimes we can go to dinner?

> *(Tommy's cell phone rings.*
> *Rings.*
> *He resists picking it up in front of Darja.)*

Pick it up.

…

…

Pick it up.

> *(It rings until it goes to voicemail. Or until he sends it to*
> *voicemail.)*

Her car costs more than you make in three years. What you think
will happen? She leave her husband for you and your Honda?
TOMMY. *(Moving to exit.)* Have a // good night.
DARJA. *(Follows after Tommy.)* She move in with you? What you
can give this woman? What you think it's so special in *you?*
TOMMY. I'm not doin this right now.

> *(Darja gets in Tommy's face, blocks his exit.)*

DARJA. You know what you—HEY!—you know what you are?
You are toy for her. Pool toy. She it's bored and there you are.
"Girlfriend"? You are fucking dreaming. You never will be for her
more. You will never be more.
TOMMY. You done?

(Darja attacks Tommy.)
(He restrains her.
Pushes her away from him.)
(They stand apart.
This has never happened before between them.)
Don't ever fuckin wonder.
DARJA. What.
TOMMY. Why yer life's been what it's been.
(Tommy moves to exit. Remembers something.)
Three weeks.
DARJA. Don't worry. Am gone tonight.
...
TOMMY. Okay then.
Take fuckin care.
(Tommy exits.)

Scene 4
2006. Fall.

Very late night. The stage should feel a little different.

Darja enters. Her face is badly bruised.

*She looks as though she's traveled a far distance from someplace.
She may have just come from across the street, from the factory,
but there is deep weathering to her.*

*She looks for some cardboard, some debris, to make a bed.
Perhaps a dirty tire is her pillow.*

*She takes her coat off, lays it down, lies on it.
It's too cold.
She puts it back on.
She takes off her scarf, lays it on the tire to cushion her face.
She is about to lay down when she remembers something.*

She takes out a small votive candle. And a lighter.

Lights it.
And places it nearby.

She does the sign of the cross.
And lies down.

A car passes.

A car stops.

And a car drives off.

A young man enters. Vic is teenage. Skull cap, hoodie, jeans.
Tattoos. He's physically frail under his many layers but he acts
like brick. He considers something in his hands as he enters.

He sees a body on the ground and quickly stuffs the thing in
his pocket.

He walks up to Darja, protective of this, his turf. He stands
over her.

VIC. 'Ey.
'Ey, man.
'Ey, man, you cool?
You cool?
You dead?
DARJA. please no
VIC. *(Seeing it's a woman.)* Oh shit.
DARJA. please
VIC. *(Seeing her face.)* Oh shit, man.
DARJA. please I have no money
VIC. Yeah, man, I figured.
Listen, yer not tryin to sleep out here tonight, are you? Cuz I'ma
tell you right now that ain't the dopest of thoughts.
DARJA. What?
VIC. 'Ey man, don't cry.
DARJA. Is just my face.
VIC. You look like you need some ice or somethin.
DARJA. No.
VIC. I could get you ice.
DARJA. Is enough cold for me.

36

VIC. QuikChek ain't far.

DARJA. No please thank you no. Thank you. I am thirty-four years old woman. I can take care myself.

VIC. Um, lady?, you nappin on a tire.*

…

Holy shit, man. Yer like… holy… shit… yer like A Battered Woman. Yer like a legit battered woman.

DARJA. Am sorry. I go.

VIC. Nah, man, nah. Sorry, I'm just, y'know, I'm like, Takin' Stock. This is some crazy shit right here I'm seein. This really happens. Shit.

(He stares at her a little too long.)

I mean, I mean if you know where to go, y'know, like a women's place or somethin, man, then go, go, you should totally go. But I mean you don't *gotta* go. *(Checks his pager/phone.)* Not yet.

(Vic spots the lit candle on the ground.)

You workin on some *ambience* there?

DARJA. What?

VIC. Shit, should I not try 'n make you laugh? It hurt yer face?

DARJA. The bus it's not coming.

VIC. What? Yeah, I know.

DARJA. Not this late.

VIC. Nope. Nope prob'ly not. Were you waitin for the bus?

DARJA. No I just say you in case *you* coming here for waiting.

VIC. Me? Man, I ain't waitin on no bus, man, nah.

DARJA. So what you come for?

VIC. Things.

Business.

Sales.

…

Things.

(He stares too long.)

DARJA. I have papers. Not with me now but I have.

VIC. I look like a cop?

DARJA. You are very questions. You very questions and little answers to be just standing here in the night waiting where is no one around to—oooooh. Oh okay. I know what you are.

VIC. Yeah? What am I?

* If tires do not factor in to your set, consider replacing the line with "rock." Or "crackpipe."

DARJA. Yeah okay I know.

VIC. Okay. Well, the thing you think I am… it bother you?

DARJA. We all of us need money.

VIC. Not a bad way to make it, I'ma tell you that.

DARJA. Yeah okay I don't think so I agree but. We are different peoples.

You say you know women's place?

VIC. I know of 'em. That they got 'em. I'd assume they would around *here*.

What's the name of the stairs fucked you up?

DARJA. Excuse?

VIC. Who fucked you up?

DARJA. Why?

VIC. Okay. You don't trust me. But so it was your husband?, boyfriend?

DARJA. Why.

VIC. Father?, yer son?

DARJA. No. Not my son. No.

VIC. O, shit! That is Fucked Up. It was your son?

DARJA. No! Not my son! Why you saying things my son! What the fuck it's your problem saying things you don't know. This it's how people gets to trouble. You kinds people you stay away my son.

…

…

…

VIC. Whoah.

Okay.

Arright, man. Okay.

But listen. I roll up to, fuckin, this place might as well be *Detroit*, at one A.M. and I see a fuckin lady turnin in on the ground. A *lady*. Fuckin, tuckin herself in on this hepatitis ground. Shiner like a, *damn*. And you want me just to roll right out like the world don't affect me?

DARJA. Why it's only for lady you stop?

VIC. Woman, are you serious?, someone could—hold up, what you mean like instead of for a man? What, you think I got like intentions?

DARJA. I don't know what you got.

VIC. Man, that's how men get into fuckin trouble. Don't be throwin no *intentions* on me. I'm talkin bout other kinds a men, the shit other kinds a men could do if they find you just laid out here like a free pile a cash. *You* would know. Right?

...

Shit, try to get you ice, try to talk, be nice'n shit. Fuck. 'N you do me like that? Tsss okay.

DARJA. Was my husband. Was my husband did to me this. Happy?

VIC. Yo but why'd he hit you? Was he drunk?

DARJA. Why you asking whole these questions me?

VIC. It happen a lot?

DARJA. Why you asking?

VIC. Yo where you from like, Russia?

DARJA. *(Offended.)* NO.

VIC. So you from like a Little Russia then like one of them Bosnias or—oh shit. OH. SHIT. Were you like... *trafficked?*

DARJA. What?

VIC. Like... *trafficked?*

... In like a sexual // kinda way?

DARJA. I used to work there. Okay? That factory. When I was working there, I remember sometimes they don't close back door when they do delivery. So I think I go there, sleep there—

VIC. You got no place to sleep?

DARJA. No yes I have but—

VIC. Gotcha. Right.

DARJA. But now some asshole he put lock so. Here I am. Don't call to no one, okay? My husband, he was my boss there. My second husband, he was boss. Before this place close. He used to manage whole that building.

VIC. And now he...?

DARJA. Does not.

How you come here? You have car maybe?

VIC. Nah, man, shit, I wish I had a car, nah. Where you need to go?

DARJA. Home.

VIC. Yeah, I'ma say that's probl'y not the best thought either.

DARJA. This was not best thought also.

VIC. You wanna get a hotel?

DARJA. Excuse?

VIC. Just, to sleep in.

DARJA. I...

... I have no money.

VIC. You need money?

(Off her look.) Whoah, man. It ain't even like that.

DARJA. How it's like so?

39

VIC. I mean, I *got* money.

DARJA. Yeah you got but… *how* you got… can't be so good.

VIC. You about to sleep in the street and you really gonna get moral on me right now, ma?

DARJA. Why you call // me this?

VIC. It's just how we do // out here, nah'mean.

DARJA. How who?, // who "we"?

VIC. Well what's yer name then. What's yer name.

(She considers.)

DARJA. Darja.

VIC. Yeah? I'm Vic.

(Vic offers her a fist bump.
A pause.
She has no idea what to do with this.
Eventually, somehow, Darja "bumps" back.
Though it's probably more a slap on the fist. Something unexpected.
This ignites a rap explosion.)

Vic Vic the Slick. Yeah, Vic the Brick. Yeah, Vic the Vic the Buttery Buttery Bisquick. I got a good name for this, right? I'm the Marinara on yer Mozzarella Stick. Corner Kick on a Hat Trick. Don't need a Sidekick OH SHIT is that a Deer Tick? Salt Lick. Toothpick. Saint Nick.

(Darja's stone serious.)

See it's just I don't wanna make you laugh, y'know, cuz a yer face. So I'm not even tryin to make you laugh.

DARJA. … Card Trick.

VIC. Politik! You lightnin' quick!

…

DARJA. … Stick.

(Darja smiles. Then grabs her face.)

Joj. ["Ow."]

VIC. Oh shit, I'm sorry. Sorry.

(Vic watches Darja holding her face, trying not to smile.)

But I'm not. I'm also not sorry. You got a good laugh.

Yo, lemme get you some ice. And a hotel. It's not terrible how I got money. Not to me.

DARJA. Why you do what you do?

VIC. I like it.

DARJA. You like doing what you do to people?

VIC. Wouldn't do it if I didn't.

DARJA. But… you are hurting people.

VIC. I mean, only if they're *into* that, nam'sayin.
I ain't tryin to *force* nobody to come to me.
And it's good conversation sometimes too. Before, y'know. Before
it gets goin. Sometimes I'm like shit, should I pay *you*?
Yeah, man. I like it.
…
So what's up, you wanna go?

DARJA. You must really need this money if—

VIC. I don't. Okay? Truth is, these men *think* they need to pay me.
I think they feel better payin, after. And, so, that's cool. Whatever.
That's cool.

DARJA. Men?

VIC. Yeah. Men. What.
Don't tell nobody. Okay?
It ain't about money for me. And anyway I don't like bein home
either so.

DARJA. Why you don't like?

VIC. Yo, you hungry? Wanna hit up a diner?

DARJA. Why you—

VIC. Look, it's not like *your* situation or anything, my house?, but
I mean… it's a different kinda shitty situation but it ain't no better
than yours.
I mean.
Shit.
I mean, it's *prob'ly* better than yours but.
There's just something very wrong there. At my house.
And if they *really*, y'know, knew about me…
…
So. Tops? Tick Tock? Yo, or we could just walk to Olympia from here.

DARJA. What these places are?

VIC. Diners.

DARJA. I never been these places.

VIC. What. You. What. You live in Jersey, right?

DARJA. Yes.

VIC. And you never been to a diner?

DARJA. No.

VIC. GIRL. There's like a third of the country's diners in Jersey and that is a FACT. Babies come out the womb suckin on Disco Fries. You seriously never been?

DARJA. Is just food, yes?

VIC. "Just"… okay. You need to come with me right now. This is real.

> *(She's not moving.)*

I got this.

DARJA. And then we go to hotel?

VIC. Yeah.

I mean NO.

I mean

nah.

I mean *you* can stay at the hotel. I'll crash maybe but that's all. I got school tomorrow.

DARJA. School?

VIC. High. High school. In the morning.

DARJA. You?

VIC. I look mad mature.

DARJA. You go to high school?

VIC. Most days, yeah.

DARJA. You know my son?

VIC. Oh shit do I? What grade he in?

DARJA. Freshman.

VIC. Oh word? I'm a junior.

Where he go?

Cuz uh I'm at Seton Hall Prep.

> *(He fishes under his shirt. Whips out a tie.*
> *Hangs it over his baggy shirt like a tongue.)*

I'ma guess he ain't at Seton Hall Prep, is he?

DARJA. You are rich?

VIC. So don't feel bad.

C'mon, some people were supposed to come get me. Not the first time they ditched me so. Whatever, y'know. I kinda got nowhere to go.

DARJA. You got home to go.

VIC. You don't wanna hang?

DARJA. What?

VIC. Spend time? Together?

DARJA. I'm thirty-four years old woman.

VIC. So?

DARJA. So you don't want to be spending your time with me.

...

VIC. You don't like my company?

DARJA. *(The truth.)* I... I am so tired.

VIC. Arright, man, so I'll just take you to a hotel. You can sleep. Call yer son.

DARJA. He's at friend's house.

VIC. Must be nice.

Friend's house.

DARJA. No. No they are not.

No.

...

VIC. He can come too.

To the hotel.

If he cute.

...

Did uh... did stuff happen to him too? To yer son? Tonight?

(She looks away.)

Yeah you ain't goin home tonight.

DARJA. No I should go. I don't even know what time it's—

VIC. It's late. C'mon. They got ice in hotels. You ever been in one?

DARJA. I clean *houses*. Not hotels.

VIC. I think you'll like it.

Or we can just go to my house. I can get us a cab. House is so big no one's even gonna know yer there. You can just crash. Sleep. Eat some breakfast. YO. I make baller fuckin pancakes. Blueberry'n shit.

DARJA. I don't know I should go—

VIC. Okay. Yer skeeved. Understandable. You don't know me. Look, I'ma just give you the money. We'll get you a hotel. And I'll walk you there. I can even drop you off like a block away if you want. I don't hafta stay if yer not good with it.

Or, here. Why don't you just, here.

(Vic takes out a wad of cash. Extends it to Darja.
Darja looks at Vic a long moment. Considering.)

For real. It's cool.

(Suddenly, Darja embraces him to her, strong.)

> *He's taken aback.*
> *But sinks into it. We see his need here too.)*

It's cool, man. No bigs.

DARJA. I can't take it.

VIC. I'm sure you can, man. Look, I was gonna pay for a hotel tonight anyway. Guys from school they can't like, toke at home obviously so. I know they only call me up so I can bankroll that shit for 'em. I usually just sit in the corner while they smoke and like, feel girls up'n shit. Most times they're too fucked up to even say Thank You.

It's just like a hundred bucks. Seriously, it's just pocket money. It's just money. You can have it.

DARJA. I can't.

VIC. Why?

> *(A car passes. It blares its horn.*
> *Vic and Darja separate.)*

Oh, shit.

Oh shit that's them.

They

shit wow

they actually showed.

DARJA. You should go.

VIC. Nah, man.

…

(Tempted.) Should I?

DARJA. You want to?

VIC. Can I?

…

DARJA. Yes.

Go.

VIC. You sure?

DARJA. I know you want to.

Be careful.

(Genuine.) Have fun.

VIC. 'Ey but, here, man. *(Re: money.)*

DARJA. No. I can't take nothing from you.

VIC. Yeah you can.

DARJA. Is okay, I can sleep behind factory—

VIC. Take it.

DARJA. —or maybe I go to diner, stay there what it's left of the night.
VIC. Just take it. They're turnin the car around.
DARJA. So you will need this for tonight.
VIC. Take it.
DARJA. No.
VIC. Cmon, I gotta go.
DARJA. No.
VIC. Give it to yer son then.

(Car horn.)

DARJA. You think this can do something?, this hundred dollars?
VIC. What?
DARJA. I sleep one night in hotel and then I what? One night I sleep and then, next day, I what? Or I go get my son, we sleep or we take bus some place and then we what? Everything will just okay? I take care myself my son.
But *I* do this.
Don't give to me money you feel bad my son.
VIC. Yo I'm just tryin to help.
DARJA. Don't give to me money so you don't feel bad.

(Car horn.)

VIC. Don't fuck him over so *you* don't feel bad.

(Car horn.)

DARJA. They will not wait so long. Go. Your friends are waiting.
VIC. Yo, if I throw this on the ground, will you take it or you gonna let it roll away?

(Car engine. Vic looks toward it. Back at Darja.)

Look over there.
DARJA. What?
VIC. Look over there. That way.

(Vic points in the opposite direction of the car of friends.)

DARJA. (Knows what he's doing.) No.
VIC. Just, c'mon, man, look over there.
"Oh shit!
Look at that moon!"
Wow.

(She hesitates.
She knows what Vic will do.)

45

But she does. She looks at the moon.

They both look at the moon a moment.

…

Then, simultaneously, Darja extends her hand, softly,
and Vic, also softly,
slips some money into her hand.

A hand-off, of sorts.
All while still looking at the moon.

They squeeze hands as a goodbye
But never look each other in the eyes.

Then Vic runs away, toward the car.
It drives off.)

(Darja, alone.
She looks down at the money in her hands.
Looks back after Vic, now gone.
And holds this stranger in her heart for a moment.

She remembers the money.
She considers.
Decides.
And takes out her phone.)

DARJA. *Halo, kochanie.* Is me. Your mom.
I'm okay.
I hope you okay.
Wherever you go.
Tonight.
I know where you go and I don't like it.
Call me back.

> *(She hangs up.*
> *Considers.*
> *Calls back.)*

Halo. Kochanie.
Don't go home tomorrow.
Tomorrow, am cleaning house in Montclair. They won't be there so
after school I want you take bus to Montclair. Meet me there. Don't

46

go home.
We figure out what we will do.
Don't go home.
We will not go home.
Okay.
Am going to diner now.
Call me back.

>   *(She hangs up.*
>   *Considers leaving.*
>   *Something stops her.)*

…

>   *(She calls again.)*

Halo.
Aleks.
Kochanie.
It's me. Your mom.
I am so fucking sorry.

…

("Bye.") Okay.

>   *(She hangs up.*
>   *She knows he won't call back.*
>   *She looks up at the sky. Dawn.*
>   *She blows out her candle.*
>   *Sits and considers just waiting here until morning.)*

…

>   *(Darja's phone rings.*
>   *She sees who's calling.*
>   *She picks it up, hurriedly.)*

Aleks?
Aleks!

Scene 5
2014. Winter.

The thaw.
Early morning, where it still looks like night.

Darja holds her phone in her hands.

Tommy enters. He's better put together than we've seen him.
He's trying.
He fixes his hair with his palm. He carries flowers wrapped in
plastic, bought at a gas station on the way here.

Tommy has thought about what he'd say for the past few hours.

TOMMY. Before you say anything… Okay, before you say anything, just lemme say:
(Nerves.) Woo. Okay.
OKAY.
I just wanna, lemme just say, I know it's been a few days. I know we haven't talked in a few days so lemme just start with, lemme just say: I'm sorry.
You can come back home.
No charge.
I could just take you home. Right now. You can quit wastin money at motels and hostel whatevers. And you can borrow my car. Any time. Where you goin? You goin to work? You get a job? Goin to work? Wanna borrow my car? You *want* my car? Shit, I can even start takin the *bus.* Try *that* out.
I got you flowers.
DARJA. Did her husband find out?
TOMMY. What?
DARJA. Is this why she leave you?
TOMMY. What're you talkin about?
DARJA. Linda's husband. Did he find out and so you are alone now? With space in the apartment? Time to buy flowers?
…

...
...
TOMMY. Will you marry me.
...
So I um I don't got a ring. There's a funny story actually for why no ring. But I *was* gonna do um—, cuz I don't want you thinkin I didn't like, *plan*. See, I was gonna, see—

> *(Tommy points his key-fob at an offstage car.*
> *Beep-Beep.*
> *Headlights.*
> *Then, staticky Springsteen... something like "Secret Garden."*)*

Bruce.
Only the best for my baby.

> *(They listen.*
> *Tommy, totally into it.*
> *Darja, not so much.)*

> *(Perhaps he inches closer to her.*
> *Perhaps he takes her hand. Or tries to.*
> *They stare ahead.*
> *They listen to the song and stand awkwardly for a long time.)*

...
Will you marry me?
...

> *(They listen to Bruce.)*

...
DARJA. My husband died.
TOMMY. What?
DARJA. Maks.

> *(Tommy turns off the Bruce.)*

My first husband.
Aleks' father.
He died.
Last night.
Aleks called me.
He it's in Chicago.
With my car.

---

* See Special Note on Songs and Recordings on copyright page.

They, apparently, he and my car and Maks, they all are in Chicago.
That's where he go.
To Maks.
Before he—
To
meet him.
TOMMY. What happened? To...
DARJA. He was sick.
TOMMY. But what... happened?
DARJA. ... He got sick.
TOMMY. Holy fuck. Holy fuck, I'm so sorry. Were you close?
DARJA. What?
TOMMY. Sorry that's, that's a stupid fuckin.
Fuck. Darja.
I'm sorry.
...
What time's yer flight?
DARJA. Flight?
TOMMY. To Chicago. You want a ride?, to the airport?
DARJA. I don't have flight.
TOMMY. So why're you here?, at the bus stop?
DARJA. I just, I just come here.
I don't know why.
This is just what I do.
...
I want to go.
TOMMY. I can take you.
DARJA. No.
TOMMY. I can help you.
DARJA. No, Tommy.
TOMMY. I can lend you the money. For a ticket. It's no problem.
But
But I could also just buy it.

      (Darja considers.)

Don't be stubborn, D.
Funerals happen once. And fast.
...
I'll buy it.
Okay?
DARJA. Fuck. I hate this.

TOMMY. It's okay.

DARJA. I don't want to be like this.

TOMMY. It's okay.

DARJA. Your insurance it's still Blue Cross Blue Shield?

...

TOMMY. Are you serious?

DARJA. Yes.

...

TOMMY. For Aleks?

...

DARJA. *(A rare nervousness.)* Yes.

...

...

TOMMY. There's co-pays.

DARJA. I can co-pay.

TOMMY. And he can only use it till he's twenty-six. After that, good luck.

DARJA. That's four years. That's good. In four years, many things can change.

TOMMY. And I dunno if rehab's covered.

DARJA. Better than nothing.

TOMMY. You think he cares about you this way?

DARJA. What?

TOMMY. You think your son would ever take care of you?

DARJA. I don't do this so he can pay me back.

TOMMY. So why then? Why all the time Aleks? How come he can—?, and you still... how come?

DARJA. You would not know how to understand this.

TOMMY. Then it doesn't exist. Everyone's capable of understandin everything. We got all the same parts. You just gotta put it in my terms.

DARJA. You would not understand.

TOMMY. You want health insurance?

DARJA. You want woman what don't leave you?

TOMMY. Sounds like there's no guarantee of that, is there.

DARJA. And it's no guarantee your Blue Cross can do anything but what I can do but try? I am not this kind of person what sits and thinks Why whole the time. He it's my son. He can do every horrible thing to me and I will look to him and say This is Mine. This is what I have in whole this world what's mine. You have your love and you give to everybody. This world it have millions peoples

51

like me, millions womens. But is only one me for him. He can't to throw this away.

TOMMY. Billions.

DARJA. What?

TOMMY. Billions of women, actually. There are actually billions of women out there. You said millions but—it's billions.

I was just doin that thing where I listen real well.

Billions. Just like you. To choose from. But you see what I'm doin here?

(He gets down on one knee.)

I don't have a ring but do you see what I'm doin? Look, I'm not a fuckin stud, okay. I know that. I'm arright. But listen. And no I don't exactly make bank. But I pay my bills. And yeah I've fucked up. Fucked around. Okay. But yer also not a model sorry and I still love the fuckin shit outta you. Yer logic's aggravation, yer English is ridiculous, and you are one straight up crazy fuckin—yer crazy, D, sometimes. But you got wonderful legs. And yer heart is good. You like goin to the movies. I LOVE goin to the movies. You need a car. I got a car. I can make you pasta. You could make me lunches. And it's good to know that someone's got the keys if I forget mine. Darja. Aleks didn't get to choose. And he hasn't. He hasn't been. Choosin. Lately. You.

I do.

And I will. Every day. Fuckin swear.

…

Yes?

…

No?

…

…

Okay.

(Tommy gets off his knee.)

Okay. Okay, I'll just drop it. I guess you can forget it. Sorry. I don't even have a ring. Not even a fuckin silver one.

(The stores don't open—I just wanna say—not this early.)

…

I knew Linda would leave. I think. In my like, heart.

They always leave. Allison. Courtney. All of 'em. Eventually.

I mean… stay. They never leave. They just stay where they always been and I gotta leave.

I go home.
But now yer not there.
And it's so—…
At least you tap my phone.
Which is fucked but.
At least you gave a fuck enough about me to tap my phone.
Which is something.
You know my mother's birthday.
Backwards.
Which is something.
I knew you'd be here.
I knew that.
Which, I think,
is something.
…
(Dropping it.) Okay.

       (Tommy moves to exit.)

DARJA. Bruce was nice.
TOMMY. Yeah?
…
… Will you marry me?
…
DARJA. Probably.
TOMMY. *(Spiking the flowers.)* YES.
DARJA. But wait. Wait. Talk to me like, terms. So you would give insurance, rent—
TOMMY. *Half* the rent once you get on yer feet.
DARJA. Okay—
TOMMY. And I'll make pasta sometimes.
DARJA. *(He makes shitty pasta.)* Okay. Insurance, half the rent. And then what you want?
TOMMY. A marriage.
DARJA. Yeah okay but I asking what you want. I get insurance and you get someone to come home to. What does not tap your phone. Unless you like that.
And—…
TOMMY. And… Aleks?
…
DARJA. And… Aleks… would not have to live with us.
He can live close, very close, but he would not have to live with us.

53

TOMMY. It's okay, we can // talk about—
DARJA. He does not *have* to live with us.
But he might. Or close.
So, okay, so all this and then you do whatever?
TOMMY. That's not a marriage, just doin whatever.
DARJA. Okay, you are never married.
Just maybe we can get all this in writing? That we will try to be nice like this to each other.
TOMMY. If we get married, that's pretty much what we're fuckin doin. Listen, I'm gonna get the car right now and drive you to the airport. This bus shit?: aggravation.
DARJA. You are never married and you never ride this bus. You don't know what's aggravation.
TOMMY. I never rode this bus cuz I never had to.
DARJA. No. No one rides this they don't have to.
TOMMY. You don't have to.
DARJA. I have to.
TOMMY. Aggravation! I'm gettin the car.

(*Heads off.*)

DARJA. Tommy.
But what this is? What would be deal?

(*He turns back.*)

TOMMY. You do things for me. I do things for you. Marriage. Like right now, I'm about to get the car and pull up and get you like it's my fuckin job. Right up to your toes. Without you even askin.
DARJA. And later I do things for you.
TOMMY. Maybe.
If you want.

(*Darja considers.*)

Can I come?
DARJA. Where?
TOMMY. To Chicago?
Can I take you?
We can drive.
…
DARJA. I did not say yes yet.
TOMMY. I know.

DARJA. So don't try to be sneaky-charming, okay. Because everything it's not all fixed.

TOMMY. I know.

DARJA. "Probably" means maybe and not yes.

TOMMY. Okay.

DARJA. I can't answer now this, your, I can't answer right now your, question.

TOMMY. Okay.

DARJA. And I will drive.

...

TOMMY. *(She's a shitty driver.)* Okay.

...

DARJA. We maybe figure something out.
Maybe.
We'll // see—

> *(Tommy's cell phone rings.*
> *Freeze.*
>
> *Ring.*
>
> ...
>
> *Tommy turns off the phone in his pocket,*
> *without even looking to see who is calling.)*

...

> *(Darja remembers*
> *and guards herself.)*

Get the car.

> *(Tommy exits.)*
>
> *(Darja stands alone, hesitant to move.)*
>
> *(She turns to go, but—)*
>
> *(Maks enters from another part of the stage.*
> *We're in the 1990s for a moment.*
> *He goes to stand with Darja.)*

MAKS. Five minutes.
Last chance.
We are here waiting already two hours. After this, it's no more buses left.

...

Four minutes.

DARJA. No, Maks.

MAKS. Why no?

DARJA. Because I have already job.

MAKS. In shit factory.

DARJA. Yes.

In shit factory.

MAKS. It's shit factories in Chicago. Jobs, many kinds jobs, in Chicago. There it's prob'ly five already waits for me. For you too can be, if // you—

DARJA. I have job.

In New Jersey.

Right there. *(Indicates factory.)*

MAKS. He it's picking you up?

DARJA. What?

MAKS. After I go? With car?

DARJA. Who?

MAKS. Nice car?

I see him talking with you this week. The boss.

He picks you up? Hm? Takes you home?

DARJA. No.

(A dig.) Am taking *bus.*

And so what we talk? He likes me. I'm great person.

MAKS. Even with little Maks he likes you? Wow. What a guy.

He knows, in few months, you will have... little...?

DARJA. Nothing it's going on with me and the— And if this it's all you think about this moment, then you got a big problem, Maks, what things you think about.

I hope Chicago will not be too cold for you.

...

...

MAKS. Just come. I still can buy for you ticket. Just come and, and you see how you like.

DARJA. Things there it's so different really?

MAKS. Yes. Yes! There, it's, in Chicago, it's—

DARJA. *You* would be different?

...

You would want what I want?

...

56

This it's not I like one place this world or some other place. Chicago or— There it's life already here, Maks. I follow you this country. This it's enough far for me—

MAKS. Okay so just one more time you come with // me—

DARJA. No, maybe now you follow me. And stay.

MAKS. *Darju*, this is last one. Last bus. I can't use tomorrow my ticket. They don't give me money back.

DARJA. So? It's just money.

MAKS. It's not just—

DARJA. You can burn money. Gone, two seconds. Money it's nothing.

MAKS. Money's it's not nothing and you know this. This has to be today.
We can talk forever this and nothing will happen, we just will be standing here.
I want this more than anything my life, how you can't see this?

> *(She looks at him.*
>
> *And she does.*
> *She does see this.*
>
> *And makes the decision to let him go.)*

DARJA. You speaking English.

MAKS. I know. I practice all the fucking time.

DARJA. Is nice.
Is good.
You will go far.

> *(Headlights.*
> *The last bus is coming.*
> *They watch it approaching.)*

MAKS. I can send you money.

DARJA. I can send *you* money. I work harder.

MAKS. *(Tries to give her money.)* Here, // take this, it's all I have—

DARJA. No!, go. No! Maks, I don't want—

MAKS. Take it. So you can buy ticket.

DARJA. No.

MAKS. Then—sing.

DARJA. What? // No.

MAKS. Sing with me. One time.

DARJA. Your bus—

MAKS. Just one time you sing with me. Then you and you and
you go have good life.
And you will have nice thing of me for remembering.
I would like my home in your mind to be nice place.

> *(Darja considers.*
> *Then, the sound of the bus readying to depart.*
> *They look toward it.)*

DARJA. Go. It's going, go.
MAKS. Darju—
DARJA. Go!

> *(Maks and Darja quickly and achingly say goodbye without words.*
> *There's no time.*
> *Maks runs after the bus.)*

> *(Maks is gone.*
> *Darja watches him leaving.*
> *Darja watches Maks in the bus, leaving forever.)*

Nie idź! Proszę cię. Ja nie mogę. Nie mogę sama. Sama nie mogę. Kochanie…

> *(Harmonica.*
> *Maks appears somewhere else in space and time.*
> *Somewhere in a different, rewritten reality.)*

> *(Maks plays a blues song, like "Sittin on Top of the World" by Howlin' Wolf.*)*

> *(The stage falls away.*
> *The smog falls away.*
> *What was once a bruised black backdrop becomes a sky full of stars.*
> *A huge moon.*
> *A beautiful night.)*

> *(Maks plays.*
> *It's wonderful.)*

> *(Darja opens her mouth to sing.*
> *Then:*

---

* See Special Note on Songs and Recordings on copyright page.

Beep-beep. Car horn.)

(The stage returns to how we've seen it. 2014.
Maks is gone.
The stars are gone.)

...

(Darja stands alone in the quiet of the present.)

...

...

(Car horn.
Darja looks toward it.
And begins to walk toward the car.
Then,
stops a moment.)

(Darja sings for herself.
It's lovely
quiet
small
and entirely un-virtuosic.)

(Singing.) fuck this bus...
oh yeah...
fuck this bus...

...

(She looks at where she is.)

(She looks at what once was.)

(She looks at where she is.)

...

...

(She exits.)

...

(Dawn.
A bus stop stands alone.)
(A day begins.)

End of Play

Polish Phonetics & Translations

*A general note: In the Polish language, the emphasis is
on the penultimate syllable of words.*

Page 17
MAKS. *(Disbelief.) No, kurdy…*
　　Pronounciation: [no, KOOR-deh]
　　Translation: "Well, damn."

MAKS. *Dobra, to dziś zrobię Ci coś // co—*
　　Pronounciation: [DOH-brah, toh jeesh ZROB-yeh chee
　　TSOSH tso]
　　Translation: "Okay, so tonight I'm gonna do something to you
　　that—" *(Unspoken: "—drives you crazy/you can't even imagine.")*

MAKS. So tonight I—
Roztopię Cię, kobieto—
　　Pronounciation: [roz-TOP-yeh cheh, kob-YEH-to]
　　Translation: literally, "I'll melt you, woman—" or, figuratively,
　　"I'm gonna get you so wet, woman—"

Page 19
MAKS. *No, Darju, ty nie rozumiesz—*
　　Pronounciation: [no, DAR-yoo, ty nyeh roz-OOM-yesh]
　　Translation: "Okay, Darja, you don't get it—"

Page 21
MAKS. *(Singing.)*
Czerwony jak cegła—
—rozgrzany jak piec,
Muszę mieć, // muszę ją mieć—
　　Pronounced: [chair-VO-neh yak TSEG-wah
　　roz-GZANY* yak pyets
　　MOOSH-eh myech, MOOSH-eh yon myech]
　　*the "rz" in *rozgrzany* sounds like the "s" in the word "pleasure"
　　Translation: "Red as a brick/hot as an oven/I've gotta have her,
　　I've gotta have her"

Page 23

MAKS. *(Looking around.)* Okay, *może teraz nie jest // najlepszy czas—*
Pronounced: [MO-zeh* TER-ahz nyeh yest nahy-LEHP-sheh chahz]
*the "ż" in *może* sounds like the "s" in the word "pleasure"
Translation: "Maybe now is not the // best time—"

Page 46

DARJA. *Halo, kochanie.* Is me. Your mom.
Pronounced: [Ko-HAN-yeh]
Translation: "My dear" or "my love." A term of endearment.

Page 58

DARJA. Go!
Nie idź! Proszę cię. Ja nie mogę. Nie mogę sama. Sama nie mogę. Kochanie...
Pronounced: [Nyeh eej! PROSH-eh chee. Yah nyeh MO-geh. Nyeh MO-geh sama. Sama nyeh MO-geh. Ko-HAN-yeh...]
Translation: "Don't go! Please. I can't. I can't alone. Alone, I can't. My love..."

PROPERTY LIST

Tote bag full of stuff
Pile of change (coins)
Delicate nightgown
Flask of liquor
Pack of cigarettes, lighter
Harmonica
2 cell phones
Debris around the bus stop
Small votive candle
Wad of cash
Bouquet of gas station flowers in cellophane
Key-fob

SOUND EFFECTS

Car driving past
Car horn honking
Harmonica playing a blues song
Car horn blaring, getting closer
Car skidding, stopping
Car door opening, slamming shut
Music playing from car, off
Bus approaching
Bus departing

NOTES
(Use this space to make notes for your production)

NOTES
(Use this space to make notes for your production)